D1343645

ANN AND FRANCO TARUSCHIO

Ice Creams and Semi Freddi

ANN AND FRANCO TARUSCHIO
Ice Creams and Semi Freddi

Photography by Philip Wilkins

WEIDENFELD & NICOLSON

Ann and Franco Taruschio

Franco Taruschio was born in the Marche region of Italy and settled in the Marches of Wales in 1963 when, with his wife Ann, he bought The Walnut Tree Inn at Llandewi Skirrid near Abergavenny. The inn has become internationally known for its superb food.

Franco has appeared on several TV food programmes, and the couple have just finished filming a series for BBC Wales, entitled *Franco and Friends: Food from the Walnut Tree*, which will be accompanied by a book of the same name. They have written three other books: *Leaves from the Walnut Tree* (1993), *Bruschetta, Crostoni, Crostini* (1995) and *Pasta al forno* (1997).

Photograph by Siân Trenberth

Contents

Two little girls of ten and twelve years of age, powdered and tightly laced into their pointed bodices, sat facing a boy of about fifteen, dressed in an orange-coloured suit with black facings and carrying a rapier, and an old lady in black (certainly the governess); all were eating large pink ices of an odd pink colour, maybe of cinnamon, rising in sharp cones from long glass goblets.

GIUSEPPE DI LAMPEDUSA
TWO STORIES AND A MEMORY, 1962

Introduction

Ice creams give pleasure to everyone, whether they are extravagant concoctions eaten on a special occasion or a simple dessert to lick from a cone walking along on a hot summer's day. Italy, my country of birth, is renowned for its ice creams. Ice cream making is still an art there, passed down from father to son, and bars specializing in artisan ice creams are to be found throughout the country. According to Caroline Liddell and Robin Weir in their book, *Ices*, one Carlo Gatti, an Italian immigrant, is reported to have been the first person to sell ice cream from a shop in London, in 1850.

Ice creams seem to have first appeared in Europe towards the end of the 17th century. Originally the ice creams were served in attractive glass cups and eaten with a shovel-like spoon. In England, further down the market, ice creams sold from street carts were presented in 'penny licks': small, stemmed glasses which were washed out and reused, the precursor of the cone.

Generally speaking, Italians do not eat ice creams after a meal. An ice cream is a social event. Italians will invite you for an ice cream in their favourite *gelateria*. A glass of water served with an espresso coffee is often taken after the ice cream, although lately the fashion is to have a glass of sparkling wine afterwards.

The great thing about homemade ice creams is that they are not just pleasant to eat, they are also good for adults and children alike, containing protein and calcium. One point I would like to stress is that when making ice cream all equipment must be spotless and only the freshest of fresh ingredients used.

The following recipes include some *semi freddi* (semi-cold), an Italian term used to describe ice creams made without an ice cream making machine. We hope you have as much pleasure making and eating them as we do.

RICOTTA IN GELATO
Ricotta ice cream

SERVES 6–8

500 ml/16 fl oz milk
250 ml/8 fl oz double cream
½ vanilla pod, split
5 egg yolks
200 g/7 oz caster sugar
200 g/7 oz ricotta
6 tablespoons Strega
   (Italian herb liqueur)
50 g/2 oz chocolate,
   finely chopped

In a heavy-bottomed saucepan, heat the milk and cream together with the vanilla pod just to boiling point; set aside.

In a bowl, beat the egg yolks and sugar together until pale and creamy. Slowly add the hot milk, beating continuously. Return the mixture to the cleaned saucepan over a medium heat and gently stir with a wooden spoon until the custard thickens enough to coat the back of the spoon. Leave to cool.

Remove the vanilla pod, then add the ricotta and beat in with a balloon whisk. Stir in the Strega. Churn in an ice cream machine. When the ice cream is almost frozen, add the chocolate and stir in evenly.

SEMIFREDDO ALL AMARETTI
Amaretti semi freddo with coffee sauce

SERVES 6–8

125 g/4 oz caster sugar
6 egg yolks
2 teaspoons instant espresso
    coffee powder, dissolved in
    a little water
500 ml/16 fl oz whipping cream
250 g/9 oz amaretti biscuits,
    coarsely chopped

To serve
coffee sauce (page 36)

Line 6 small moulds or a 900 g/2 lb loaf tin with cling film. Put the sugar in a saucepan with 100 ml/3½ fl oz water, bring to the boil and boil for 2 minutes.

In a large bowl, beat the egg yolks with an electric beater until pale and creamy. Slowly add the hot syrup, beating continuously, then beat in the coffee; the mixture should be thick and creamy. Leave to cool.

Whip the cream until thick, but not too stiff. Add the amaretti and the whipped cream to the coffee mixture and fold in thoroughly. Divide the mixture between the lined moulds and freeze for at least 6 hours.

To serve, turn out on to individual plates and pour the coffee sauce around the semi freddi.

GELATO DI CANNELLA
Cinnamon ice cream

MAKES 2.3 LITRES/4 PINTS

600 ml/1 pint milk
300 ml/10 fl oz Jersey
    or double cream
4 cinnamon sticks
15 egg yolks
350 g/13 oz caster sugar

In a heavy-bottomed saucepan, heat the milk and cream together with the cinnamon just to boiling point; set aside.

In a bowl, beat the egg yolks and sugar together until pale and creamy. Slowly add the hot milk, stirring all the time with a wooden spoon. Return the mixture to the cleaned saucepan over a low heat and stir gently until the custard thickens enough to coat the back of the spoon. Strain the custard into a clean bowl and leave to cool.

Churn in an ice cream machine.

SEMIFREDDO DI CASSATA
Cassata semi freddo with strawberry sauce

SERVES 6–8

50 g/2 oz egg whites (2 small
  eggs or 1 large egg)
125 g/4 oz sugar
25 g/1 oz pistachio nuts,
  chopped
25 g/1 oz candied fruits,
  chopped
50 g/2 oz hazelnut brittle
  (page 37), finely chopped
1 tablespoon sultanas
250 ml/8 fl oz double cream

Strawberry sauce
150 g/5 oz very ripe strawberries
25 g/1 oz caster sugar

For the sauce, purée the strawberries with the caster sugar and then pass the mixture through a fine sieve to make a smooth sauce. Cover and store in the refrigerator.

Line a 900 g/2 lb loaf tin with cling film.

Beat the egg whites until stiff. In a heavy-bottomed saucepan, heat the sugar to 120°C/250°F or the hard ball stage. (If you do not have a sugar thermometer, test by dropping a little syrup into a bowl of iced water, then kneading it between your fingers: it should form a firm, pliable ball.) Slowly pour the hot syrup on to the egg whites, whisking all the time. Continue whisking until the meringue is cold.

Add the pistachios, candied fruits, hazelnut brittle and sultanas to the meringue and fold in well. Whip the cream until very thick, but not too stiff, then fold into the mixture. Pour into the lined tin and freeze for 5 hours. Serve sliced, with the strawberry sauce.

STRACCIATTELLA
Rich vanilla ice cream with chocolate chips

MAKES 2.3 LITRES/4 PINTS

1.2 litres/2 pints milk
15 egg yolks
350 g/13 oz caster sugar
1 vanilla pod, split
350 ml/13 fl oz whipping cream
125 g/4 oz chocolate,
    finely chopped

In a heavy-bottomed saucepan, heat the milk with the vanilla pod just to boiling point; set aside.

In a bowl, beat the egg yolks and sugar together until pale and creamy. Slowly add the hot milk, stirring all the time with a wooden spoon. Return the mixture to the cleaned saucepan over a low heat and stir gently until the custard thickens enough to coat the back of the spoon. Strain the custard into a clean bowl and leave to cool, preferably over ice.

Whip the cream until thick, but not too stiff, then fold into the custard. Churn the mixture in an ice cream machine. When the ice cream is almost frozen, add the chocolate and stir in evenly.

Semifreddo allo zabaione
Semi freddo with Marsala

SERVES 4–6

8 egg yolks
200 g/7 oz caster sugar
250 ml/8 fl oz dry Marsala
500 ml/16 fl oz double cream

Line a 900 g/2 lb loaf tin with cling film.

Put the egg yolks and sugar in a large bowl and whisk until they are thick, creamy and almost white. Add the Marsala, 1 tablespoon at a time, whisking well after each addition.

Place the bowl over a saucepan of barely simmering water and continue whisking the mixture until it is stiff. Transfer the mixture to a clean bowl and leave until cold, stirring from time to time.

Whip the cream until thick, but not too stiff, then gently fold into the egg mixture. Pour into the lined tin and freeze for 5–6 hours.

GELATO ALLA GIANDUIA
Chocolate and hazelnut ice cream

MAKES 2.3 LITRES/4 PINTS

600 ml/1 pint milk
300 ml/10 fl oz Jersey
 or double cream
1 vanilla pod, split
15 egg yolks
350 g/13 oz caster sugar

Gianduia paste
200 g/7 oz skinned hazelnuts
 (page 37)
50 g/2 oz pure cocoa powder

For the gianduia paste, roast the hazelnuts until deep brown, but not burnt. Put the nuts into a food processor and grind until the oil runs from the nuts. Add the cocoa powder and process until a paste forms.

In a heavy-bottomed saucepan, heat the milk and cream together with the vanilla pod just to boiling point; set aside.

In a bowl, beat the egg yolks and sugar together until pale and creamy. Slowly add the hot milk, stirring all the time with a wooden spoon. Return the mixture to the cleaned saucepan over a low heat and stir gently until the custard thickens enough to coat the back of the spoon. Strain into a clean cold bowl and leave until cold, preferably over ice.

Add the gianduia paste a little at a time until it has all been incorporated into the custard. Churn in an ice cream machine.

GELATO DI CARAMELLO PRALINATO
Caramel ice cream with praline

MAKES 2.3 LITRES/4 PINTS

600 ml/1 pint milk
400 ml/14 fl oz Jersey
   or double cream
500 g/1 lb 2 oz caster sugar
15 egg yolks

Praline
a little vegetable oil
125 g/4 oz sugar
125 g/4 oz whole almonds

For the praline, brush a baking sheet with vegetable oil to coat evenly. Put the sugar in a heavy-bottomed saucepan over a very low heat, and do not stir until the sugar starts to melt. As soon as the sugar has liquefied and turned to a caramel colour, add the almonds and stir in. Taking great care, as it is very hot, pour the mixture on to the oiled baking sheet and leave to harden.

Heat the milk and cream together to boiling point; set aside.

Caramelize the sugar as for the praline, then add the hot milk and cream to the caramel – never the other way round – stirring all the time.

In a bowl, beat the egg yolks together lightly. Slowly add the milk and caramel mixture to the egg yolks, stirring continuously with a wooden spoon. Return the mixture to the cleaned saucepan over a low heat and stir continuously until the caramel custard thickens enough to coat the back of the spoon. Leave to cool.

Churn in an ice cream machine. When the ice cream is almost frozen, crush the praline and fold in.

Gelato di fragole e yogurt
Strawberry and yogurt ice cream

SERVES 6–8

500 g/1 lb 2 oz strawberries
125 g/4 oz caster sugar
1 tablespoon strained
   lemon juice
200 g/7 oz full cream yogurt
4 tablespoons milk
finely grated zest of 1 lemon

Wash the strawberries with the stalks on and pat dry on paper towels. Hull the strawberries and purée them, then pass through a fine, non-metallic sieve. Add half of the sugar and the lemon juice to the purée.

In a bowl, mix the yogurt with the remaining sugar, milk and grated lemon zest, beating with a balloon whisk. Add the strawberry purée and mix well. Churn the mixture in an ice cream machine.

This refreshing gelato is not a true ice cream but is very good for people who cannot eat eggs.

GELATO DI MIELE E NOCI
Honey and walnut ice cream

SERVES 6–8

85 g/3 oz sugar
85 g/3 oz walnuts
6 egg yolks
300 ml/10 fl oz milk
6 tablespoons clear honey

Brush a baking sheet with vegetable oil to coat evenly. Put the sugar in a heavy-bottomed saucepan over a very low heat, and do not stir until the sugar starts to melt. As soon as the sugar has liquefied and turned to a caramel colour, add the walnuts and stir in. Taking great care, as it is very hot, pour the mixture on to the oiled baking sheet and leave to harden.

In a bowl set over a pan of gently simmering water, beat the egg yolks with a balloon whisk until thickened. Meanwhile, heat the milk and honey together to boiling point. Slowly add the hot milk to the eggs, stirring continuously. Return the mixture to the saucepan over a low heat and stir gently with a wooden spoon until the custard thickens enough to coat the back of the spoon. Leave to cool.

Churn in an ice cream machine. When the ice cream is almost frozen, crush the walnut praline and fold into the ice cream.

GELATO DI CAPPUCCINO
Cappuccino ice cream

MAKES 2.3 LITRES/4 PINTS

250 ml/8 fl oz milk
500 ml/16 fl oz double cream
3 teaspoons instant espresso
  coffee powder
10 egg yolks
150 g/5 oz caster sugar

To serve
whipped cream
powdered chocolate

In a heavy-bottomed saucepan, bring the milk, cream and coffee to the boil; set aside.

In a bowl, beat the egg yolks and sugar together until pale and creamy. Slowly add the hot milk, stirring continuously with a balloon whisk. Return the mixture to the cleaned saucepan over a low heat and stir with a wooden spoon until the custard thickens enough to coat the back of the spoon. Strain the custard into a bowl and leave to cool.

Churn in an ice cream machine. Serve with fresh whipped cream and a sprinkling of powdered chocolate.

SEMIFREDDO AL TORRONE
Semi freddo with nougat

SERVES 4

2 eggs, separated
2 tablespoons caster sugar
250 ml/8 fl oz double cream
2 tablespoons rum
200 g/7 oz hard torrone
   (nougat), broken into
   small pieces

Beat the egg yolks and sugar together until pale and fluffy. In separate bowls, whisk the cream and the egg whites until stiff. Add the whipped cream to the egg and sugar mixture and fold in lightly but evenly, followed by the rum. Delicately fold in the whisked egg whites and finally the pieces of nougat. Pour the mixture into custard cups or parfait dishes and freeze for at least 3 hours.

Remove from the freezer 15 minutes before serving.

The Basics

LE CIALDE DOLCE
(Cones)

MAKES 10

150 g/5 oz butter
3 tablespoons caster sugar
3 eggs, separated
6 tablespoons plain flour
extra virgin olive oil
salt

For this recipe an Italian waffle iron is needed (electric ones are available). These have shallow round moulds about 18 cm/7 inches in diameter, and are marked with a criss-cross or 'waffle' pattern. They are sold in specialist kitchen shops and catering suppliers.

Remove the butter from the refrigerator 1 hour before you need it. Cut it into small cubes and leave in a bowl to soften.

Using a wooden spoon, beat the butter until it forms a smooth cream. Add the sugar and beat in. Add the egg yolks one at a time, beating with a balloon whisk to form a soft paste. Whisk the egg whites until stiff, then delicately fold them into the mixture using a metal spoon.

Heat a waffle iron on both sides over a medium heat. Brush the iron with olive oil. Spread a 2 mm/$\frac{1}{16}$ inch thick layer of the paste over the waffle iron. Close the iron, put it on the heat and cook for 1 minute on each side. Remove the cialde with the point of a knife and form into a cone while still hot.

Cialde di zenzero
(Ginger snaps)

MAKES ABOUT 25–30

125 g/4 oz butter
100 g/3½ oz plain flour
2 teaspoons powdered ginger
225 g/8 oz caster sugar
100 g/3½ oz golden syrup

Using an electric mixer, mix the butter, flour and ginger until evenly blended. Weigh the sugar and weigh the golden syrup on top of the sugar: this way you do not lose any of the syrup. Pour the sugar and syrup into the butter and flour mixture and beat together. Pour the sticky paste on to a piece of cling film and wrap. Leave the mixture to set in the refrigerator for at least 1 hour.

Preheat the oven to 180°C/350°F/Gas Mark 4 and thoroughly grease two baking sheets.

Roll the mixture into walnut-sized balls. Put five at a time on to one of the baking sheets, spaced well apart, and bake for 8–10 minutes or until golden. Put a second batch of biscuits into the oven when the first batch is done, but leave the first batch to cool on the baking sheet for about 5 minutes, then use a palette knife to lift the biscuits on to a wire rack and leave to cool completely.

SALSA AL CAFFÈ
(Coffee sauce)

SERVES 6

300 ml/10 fl oz milk
3 teaspoons instant espresso
    coffee powder
3 egg yolks
50 g/2 oz caster sugar

In a heavy-bottomed saucepan, bring the milk and coffee to the boil; set aside.

In a bowl, beat the egg yolks and sugar together until pale and creamy. Pour the hot milk on to the egg mixture, stirring all the time. Return the sauce to the cleaned saucepan and cook over a low heat, stirring until thickened.

PAVLOVA MERINGUES

**MAKES 14 SMALL OR 24 LARGE
MERINGUES**

12 egg whites
675 g/1½ lb caster sugar
2 teaspoons cornflour
2 teaspoons white wine vinegar
2 teaspoons vanilla essence

With all the egg yolks used for ice cream making, you will have plenty of whites left over for meringues, which happen to go very well with ice cream.

Preheat the oven to its lowest setting – about 110°C/225°F/Gas Mark ¼.

Using an electric mixer, whisk the egg whites with 325 g/12 oz of the sugar until stiff. Mix the remaining sugar with the cornflour and add a little at a time to the egg whites, whisking all the time. Finally beat in the vinegar and vanilla essence. The mixture should now be so thick you can turn the bowl upside down without any of the mixture falling out.

Put spoonfuls of the mixture on to a baking sheet lined with lightly oiled nonstick baking paper, and bake for about 4 hours. The meringues should be crisp and very lightly tinted on the outside, yet remain soft and marshmallow-like in the centre.

TO SKIN HAZELNUTS

If your hazelnuts are still in their skins, spread them on a baking sheet and preheat the oven to 180°C/350°F/Gas Mark 4. Roast the nuts in the oven for 8–10 minutes, turning them after 5 minutes. Tip them on to a clean tea towel and rub until the skins flake off.

HAZELNUT BRITTLE

85 g/3 oz hazelnuts, skinned
85 g/3 oz sugar

Brush a baking sheet with vegetable oil to coat evenly. Put the sugar in a heavy-bottomed saucepan over a very low heat and heat gently, without stirring, until the sugar starts to melt. As soon as the sugar has liquefied and turned a caramel colour, add the hazelnuts and stir in. Pour the mixture on to the oiled baking sheet and leave to cool and harden.

Classic Cooking

STARTERS
Lesley Waters A former chef and now a popular television cook, appearing regularly on *Ready Steady Cook* and *Can't Cook Won't Cook*. Author of several cookery books.

VEGETABLE SOUPS
Elisabeth Luard Cookery writer for the *Sunday Telegraph Magazine* and author of *European Peasant Food* and *European Festival Food*, which won a Glenfiddich Award.

GOURMET SALADS
Sonia Stevenson The first woman chef in the UK to be awarded a Michelin star, at the Horn of Plenty in Devon. Author of *The Magic of Saucery* and *Fresh Ways with Fish*.

FISH AND SHELLFISH
Gordon Ramsay Chef/proprietor of London's Aubergine restaurant, recently awarded its second Michelin star, and author of Glenfiddich Award-winning *A Passion for Flavour*.

CHICKEN, DUCK AND GAME
Nick Nairn Chef/patron of Braeval restaurant near Aberfoyle in Scotland, whose BBC-TV series *Wild Harvest* was last summer's most successful cookery series, accompanied by a book.

LIVERS, SWEETBREADS AND KIDNEYS
Simon Hopkinson Former chef/patron at London's Bibendum restaurant, columnist and author of *Roast Chicken and Other Stories* and *The Prawn Cocktail Years*.

VEGETARIAN
Rosamond Richardson Author of several vegetarian titles, including *The Great Green Cookbook* and *Food from Green Places*.

PASTA
Joy Davies One of the creators of *BBC Good Food Magazine*, she has been food editor of *She, Woman* and *Options* and written for the *Guardian, Daily Telegraph* and *Harpers & Queen*.

CHEESE DISHES
Rose Elliot The UK's most successful vegetarian cookery writer and author of many books, including *Not Just a Load of Old Lentils* and *The Classic Vegetarian Cookbook*.

POTATO DISHES
Patrick McDonald Former chef/patron of the acclaimed Epicurean restaurant in Cheltenham, and food consultant to Sir Rocco Forte Hotels.

BISTRO
Anne Willan Founder and director of La Varenne Cookery School in Burgundy and West Virginia. Author of many books and a specialist in French cuisine.

ITALIAN
Anna Del Conte Author of several books on Italian food, including *The Gastronomy of Italy, Secrets from an Italian Kitchen* and *The Classic Food of Northern Italy* (chosen as the 1996 Guild of Food Writers Book of the Year).

VIETNAMESE

Nicole Routhier One of the United States'
most popular cookery writers, her books
include *Cooking Under Wraps, Nicole Routhier's
Fruit Cookbook* and the award-winning *The
Foods of Vietnam.*

MALAYSIAN

Jill Dupleix One of Australia's best known
cookery writers and broadcasters, with columns
in the *Sydney Morning Herald* and *Elle.* Her
books include *New Food* and *Allegro al dente.*

PEKING CUISINE

Helen Chen Author of *Chinese Home Cooking,*
she learned to cook traditional Peking dishes
from her mother, Joyce Chen, the *grande dame* of
Chinese cooking in the United States.

STIR-FRIES

Kay Fairfax A writer and broadcaster whose
books include *100 Great Stir-fries, Homemade*
and *The Australian Christmas Book.*

NOODLES

Terry Durack Australia's most widely read
restaurant critic and co-editor of the *Sydney
Morning Herald Good Food Guide.* He is the
author of *YUM,* a book of stories and recipes.

NORTH INDIAN CURRIES

Pat Chapman Founded the Curry Club in
1982. A regular broadcaster on television and
radio, he is the author of 20 books, which have
sold more than 1 million copies.

GRILLS AND BARBECUES

Brian Turner Chef/patron of Turner's in
Knightsbridge and one of Britain's most
popular food broadcasters; he appears
frequently on *Ready Steady Cook, Food and
Drink* and many other television programmes.

SUMMER AND WINTER CASSEROLES

Anton Edelmann Maître Chef des Cuisines
at the Savoy Hotel, London. Author of
six cookery books, he has also appeared
on television.

TRADITIONAL PUDDINGS

Tessa Bramley Chef/patron of the
acclaimed Old Vicarage restaurant in Ridgeway,
Derbyshire and author of *The Instinctive Cook.*

DECORATED CAKES

Jane Asher Author of several cookery books
and a novel. She has also appeared in her own
television series, *Jane Asher's Christmas* (1995).

FAVOURITE CAKES

Mary Berry One of Britain's leading cookery
writers, her numerous books include *Mary
Berry's Ultimate Cake Book.* She has made many
television and radio appearances.

ICE CREAMS AND SEMI FREDDI

Ann and Franco Taruschio Owners of the
renowned Walnut Tree Inn near Abergavenny
in Wales, soon to appear in a television series,
Franco and Friends: Food from the Walnut Tree.
They have written three books together.

Text © Ann and Franco Taruschio 1997

Ann and Franco Taruschio have asserted their right to
be identified as the authors of this Work.

Photographs © Philip Wilkins 1997

First published in 1997 by
George Weidenfeld & Nicolson
The Orion Publishing Group
Orion House
5 Upper St Martin's Lane
London WC2H 9EA

All rights reserved. No part of this publication
may be reproduced, stored in a retrieval system, or
transmitted in any form or by any means, electronic,
mechanical or otherwise, without prior permission
of the copyright holder.

British Library Cataloguing-in-Publication data
A catalogue record for this book is available from
the British Library

ISBN 0 297 82337 X

Designed by Lucy Holmes
Edited by Maggie Ramsay
Food styling by Bridget Sargeson
Typesetting by Tiger Typeset